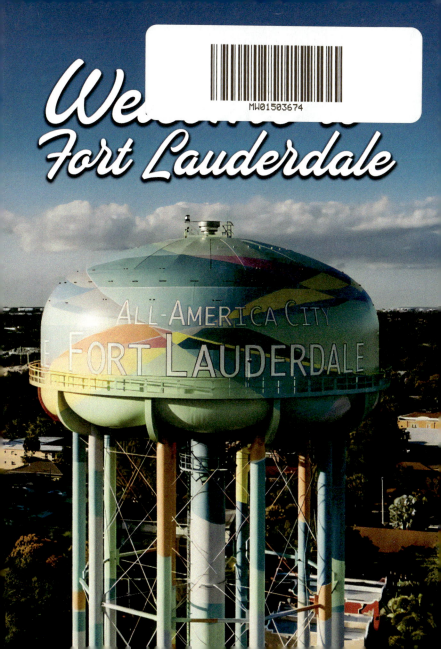

Welcome to Fort Lauderdale

Introduction

WHAT MAKES FORT LAUDERDALE SO SPECIAL?

THE CITY OF FORT LAUDERDALE IS KNOWN WORLDWIDE FOR MANY THINGS.
FIRST, ITS NICKNAME "THE VENICE OF AMERICA" COMES FROM THE 165 MILES OF SCENIC INLAND WATERWAYS THAT WIND THROUGH THE CITY. SECOND, IT'S KNOWN AS "THE YACHTING CAPITAL OF THE WORLD" FOR ITS BOATING ACTIVITIES, INCLUDING BOAT PARADES AND THE FORT LAUDERDALE INTERNATIONAL BOAT SHOW (FLIBS), WHICH IS THE LARGEST IN-WATER BOAT SHOW IN THE WORLD! THIRD, ITS STUNNING BEACHES AND BEAUTIFUL YEAR-ROUND WEATHER MAKE IT A PERFECT VACATION DESTINATION AND SPRING BREAK HOT-SPOT. FOURTH, ITS DIVERSE ART CULTURE, NIGHTLIFE, AND FOOD SCENE MAKE IT A VERY UNIQUE AMERICAN CITY!

FORT LAUDERDALE GUIDE BOOK AIMS TO MAKE YOUR EXPLORATION OF THIS CITY EASY & FUN! WHETHER YOU ARE HERE FOR A SHORT TIME OR A LOCAL EXPLORING YOUR OWN BACKYARD, THIS BOOK WILL BREAK DOWN THE MUST-DO'S, MUST-SEE'S & MUST-EAT'S IN THE CITY!

CONTENTS

Before you go

BASIC INFO

STATE: FLORIDA
COUNTY: BROWARD COUNTY

TIME ZONE
EASTERN STANDARD TIME (GMT-5)

CURRENCY
US DOLLAR (USD / $)
EXCHANGE RATE $1 = €0.92

WEATHER

MONTH	HIGH / LOW(°F)	RAIN
JANUARY	76° / 60°	5 DAYS
FEBRUARY	78° / 62°	5 DAYS
MARCH	80° / 65°	5 DAYS
APRIL	83° / 68°	5 DAYS
MAY	86° / 73°	8 DAYS
JUNE	88° / 76°	12 DAYS
JULY	90° / 77°	12 DAYS
AUGUST	91° / 77°	12 DAYS
SEPTEMBER	89° / 77°	13 DAYS
OCTOBER	86° / 74°	10 DAYS
NOVEMBER	81° / 68°	7 DAYS
DECEMBER	78° / 64°	6 DAYS

PUBLIC TRANSPORTATION

AMTRAK
BROWARD COUNTY TRANSIT (BCT)
BRIGHTLINE
B-CYCLE/AVMED RIDES
UBER/LYFT
COMMUNITY SHUTTLE (LAUDERGO)
TRI-RAIL
WATER TAXI
CIRCUIT

USEFUL WEBSITES

CITY TRANSPORTATION
WWW.FORTLAUDERDALE.GOV/GOVERNMENT/DEPARTMENTS-I-Z
/TRANSPORTATION-AND-MOBILITY/TRANSPORTATION-DIVISION

AIRPORT TRANSPORTATION
WWW.BROWARD.ORG/AIRPORT

ATTRACTIONS & EVENTS
WWW.VISITLAUDERDALE.COM

ATTRACTIONS & EVENTS
HTTPS://WWW.GORIVERWALK.COM/EVENTS/
GREATER-FORT-LAUDERDALE-EVENT-CALENDAR

IMPORTANT PHONE #S

FOR NON-EMERGENCY POLICE OR FIRE ASSISTANCE IN FORT LAUDERDALE, CALL 954-764-HELP (4357)

EMERGENCY: CALL 911 FOR LIFE-THREATENING SITUATIONS, TO STOP A CRIME, OR REPORT A FIRE.

REPORT A CRIME TIP: 954-493-TIPS (8477)

GENERAL INFORMATION: 954-765-4321

REPORT ABUSE: 1-800-96-ABUSE (22873)

BROWARD SHERIFF'S OFFICE (BSO) CENTRAL BROWARD DISTRICT OFFICE (NON-EMERGENCY): 954-321-4800

STATION 14 (NON-EMERGENCY): 954-791-1058

STATION 23 (NON-EMERGENCY): 954-791-1055

FIXIT FTL (CUSTOMER SERVICE): 954-828-8000

FORT LAUDERDALE POLICE DEPARTMENT (FLPD) ONLINE INCIDENT REPORTING SYSTEM:
HTTPS://WWW.FLPD.GOV/COMMUNITY-RESOURCES/ONLINE-INCIDENT-REPORTING

THIS BOOK WILL SAVE YOU MONEY!

DEAL

LOOK FOR PAGES WITH GOLDEN CORNERS

BEYOND BEING AN INFORMATIONAL GUIDE TO THE CITY THE FORT LAUDERDALE GUIDE BOOK IS A COLLABORATION OF 50+ LOCAL BUSINESSES BRINGING YOU DEALS & DISCOUNTS TO HELP EXPERIENCE THE BEST THIS CITY HAS TO OFFER!

HOW IT WORKS:

1. VISIT ANY FEATURED BUSINESS THAT HAS A "DEAL SQUARE" IN THE BOOK

2. SHOW YOUR GUIDE BOOK

3. ENJOY SOMETHING FREE OR DISCOUNTED THANKS TO A LOCAL FTL BUSINESS!

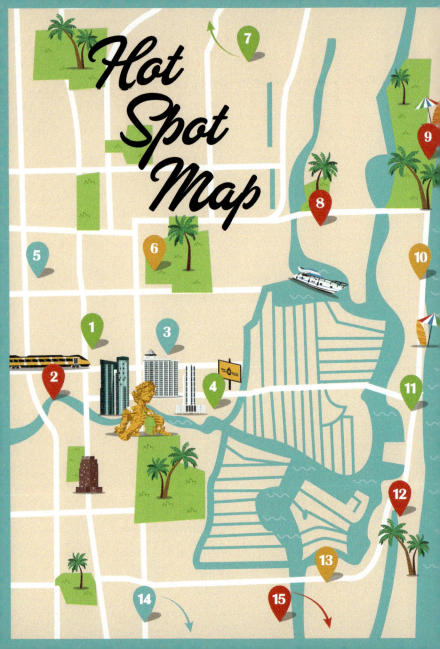

Hot Spot Map

1. **THE BRIGHTLINE STATION** – 101 NW 2ND AVE, FORT LAUDERDALE
HIGH SPEED PASSENGER TRAIN TO MIAMI, WEST PALM, ORLANDO & MORE!

2. **THE RIVERWALK** – 400 SW 2ND ST, FORT LAUDERDALE
SCENIC WALKWAY ALONG THE NEW RIVER

3. **DOWNTOWN FORT LAUDERDALE** – 32 E LAS OLAS BLVD, FORT LAUDERDALE
A VIBRANT, URBAN AREA KNOWN FOR ITS MIX OF SHOPPING, DINING, AND CULTURE

4. **LAS OLAS BLVD** – 601 E LAS OLAS BLVD, FORT LAUDERDALE
FORT LAUDERDALES MOST FAMOUS STREET FOR DINING & SHOPPING

5. **THRIVE ART DISTRICT** – 710 NW 5TH AVE, FORT LAUDERDALE
5-ACRE CULTURAL AND ARTISTIC ENCLAVE HOME OF THE FORT LAUDERDALE ART WALK

6. **HOLIDAY PARK** – 601 E LAS OLAS BLVD, FORT LAUDERDALE
HOME OF THE PARKER, THE FTL WAR MEMORIAL & THE BAPTIST HEALTH ICEPLEX

7. **CHASE STADIUM** – 1350 NW 55TH ST, FORT LAUDERDALE
HOME OF INTER MIAMI FC & THE MIAMI SHARKS RUGBY

8. **THE GALLERIA MALL** – 2414 E SUNRISE BLVD, FORT LAUDERDALE
ONE OF SOUTH FLORIDA'S PREMIER SHOPPING CENTER DESTINATIONS

9. **HUGH TAYLOR BIRCH** – 3109 E SUNRISE BLVD, FORT LAUDERDALE
POPULAR FLORIDA STATE PARK – A VIEW OF PREHISTORIC FORT LAUDERDALE

10. **BONNET HOUSE MUSEUM** – 900 N BIRCH RD, FORT LAUDERDALE
HISTORIC HOME, MUSEUM & GARDEN

11. **FORT LAUDERDALE BEACH** – 240 LAS OLAS CIR, FORT LAUDERDALE
WIDE, EXPANSIVE SHORELINE WITH PRISTINE WATERS – THE GEM OF OUR CITY

12. **MARINA VILLAGE** – 849 SEABREEZE BLVD, FORT LAUDERDALE
OPEN AIR FOOD HALL WITH WATERFRONT VIEWS

13. **BROWARD COUNTY CONVENTION CENTER** – 1950 EISENHOWER BLVD
SOUTH FLORIDA'S POPULAR EVENT DESTINATION

14. **FLL AIRPORT** – 100 TERMINAL DR, FORT LAUDERDALE
INTERNATIONAL AIRPORT NONSTOP SERVICE TO 125+ DESTINATIONS

15. **FORT LAUDERDALE TERMINAL** – 1850 ELLER DR, FORT LAUDERDALE
THE SEAPORT OF FORT LAUDERDALE

Short Trip Must Do's

ONLY IN FORT LAUDERDALE
FOR A SHORT TIME?

HERE ARE 8 MUST DO & MUST SEE GEMS THAT MAKE FORT LAUDERDALE SPECIAL

"FLORIDA'S OCEAN FRONT GEM"

FORT LAUDERDALE BEACH

FORT LAUDERDALE BEACH, OFTEN CALLED THE "VENICE OF AMERICA," IS ONE OF FLORIDA'S MOST ICONIC COASTAL DESTINATIONS. LOCATED ALONG THE ATLANTIC OCEAN IN BROWARD COUNTY, THIS BEAUTIFUL BEACH STRETCHES FOR SEVEN MILES WITH ITS SIGNATURE WAVE WALL AND PROMENADE THAT SEPARATES THE SHORE FROM THE PALM-LINED A1A HIGHWAY. THE BEACH IS ACCESSIBLE YEAR-ROUND, WITH ITS PEAK SEASON RUNNING FROM NOVEMBER THROUGH APRIL. TEMPERATURES TYPICALLY RANGE FROM 65-85°F. SUMMER MONTHS BRING WARMER TEMPERATURES (80-95°F) WITH HIGHER HUMIDITY AND OCCASIONAL AFTERNOON THUNDERSTORMS.

LAS OLAS BLVD

LAS OLAS BOULEVARD IS KNOWN AS FORT LAUDERDALE'S PRIME DESTINATION FOR SHOPPING, DINING, AND CULTURAL EXPERIENCES. STRETCHING APPROXIMATELY 2.5 MILES FROM DOWNTOWN FORT LAUDERDALE EASTWARD TO THE ATLANTIC OCEAN, THIS HISTORIC THOROUGHFARE SERVES AS BOTH THE COMMERCIAL AND CULTURAL HEART OF THE CITY.

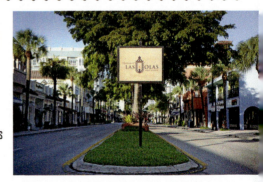

LAS OLAS IS HOME TO MORE THAN 120 SPECIALTY RETAIL STORES, ART GALLERIES, AND FASHION BOUTIQUES. UNLIKE CONVENTIONAL SHOPPING MALLS, LAS OLAS OFFERS A CURATED MIX OF INDEPENDENT RETAILERS AND DESIGNER BRANDS IN AN OUTDOOR SETTING.

THE BOULEVARD'S DINING SCENE FEATURES OVER 40 RESTAURANTS, RANGING FROM CASUAL SIDEWALK CAFÉS TO UPSCALE DINING ESTABLISHMENTS. CUISINE OPTIONS SPAN THE GLOBE FROM AUTHENTIC ITALIAN AND MEDITERRANEAN TO CONTEMPORARY AMERICAN AND INNOVATIVE FUSION CONCEPTS. MANY RESTAURANTS OFFER AL FRESCO SEATING, ALLOWING DINERS TO ENJOY FLORIDA'S BEAUTIFUL WEATHER, NO MATTER THE TIME OF YEAR.

FORT LAUDERDALE RIVERWALK

FORT LAUDERDALE'S RIVERWALK IS A SCENIC BRICK-PAVED WALKWAY STRETCHING ALONG THE NEW RIVER IN DOWNTOWN FORT LAUDERDALE, FLORIDA. THIS WATERFRONT ATTRACTION HAS BECOME A CULTURAL AND RECREATIONAL CORNERSTONE OF THE CITY, EARNING IT THE NICKNAME "FLORIDA'S MOST BEAUTIFUL MILE."

FOR VISITORS TO FORT LAUDERDALE, THE RIVERWALK SHOWS OFF WHAT MAKES FORT LAUDERDALE SPECIAL. IT'S A PERFECT MIX OF NATURAL BEAUTY, CULTURE, AND DOWNTOWN CITY LIFE, ALL WRAPPED AROUND THE WATERWAYS THAT GIVE THE CITY ITS "VENICE OF AMERICA" NICKNAME.

THE RIVERWALK IS FREE AND OPEN TO THE PUBLIC 24 HOURS A DAY!

FORT LAUDERDALE WATER TAXI

THE FORT LAUDERDALE WATER TAXI OFFERS ONE OF THE MOST ENJOYABLE WAYS TO EXPERIENCE "THE VENICE OF AMERICA," PROVIDING BOTH TRANSPORTATION AND SIGHTSEEING ALONG THE CITY'S WATERWAYS. THIS SERVICE HAS BECOME AN ESSENTIAL PART OF FORT LAUDERDALE'S CHARM AND APPEAL TO VISITORS AND RESIDENTS ALIKE. THE SERVICE OPERATES DAILY, TYPICALLY FROM AROUND 10 AM UNTIL LATE EVENING, WITH EXTENDED HOURS DURING PEAK TOURIST SEASONS AND SPECIAL EVENTS.

BONNET HOUSE MUSEUM & GARDENS

LOCATED BETWEEN THE ATLANTIC OCEAN AND THE INTRACOASTAL WATERWAY IN FORT LAUDERDALE, THE BONNET HOUSE MUSEUM & GARDENS STANDS AS A TESTAMENT TO ART, ARCHITECTURE, AND NATURAL CONSERVATION. THIS 35-ACRE HISTORIC ESTATE OFFERS VISITORS A GLIMPSE INTO FLORIDA'S PAST WHILE SHOWCASING BEAUTIFUL BOTANICAL GARDENS, ART COLLECTIONS, AND UNIQUE ARCHITECTURAL ELEMENTS.

THE PROPERTY'S HISTORY BEGINS WITH HUGH TAYLOR BIRCH, A CHICAGO ATTORNEY WHO PURCHASED THE LAND IN 1895 AS A WEDDING GIFT FOR HIS DAUGHTER HELEN AND HER HUSBAND, ARTIST FREDERIC CLAY BARTLETT. AFTER HELEN'S UNTIMELY DEATH IN 1925, FREDERIC MARRIED EVELYN FORTUNE LILLY, AND TOGETHER THEY TRANSFORMED THE PROPERTY INTO THE BEAUTIFUL AND ARTISTIC ESTATE VISITORS SEE TODAY.

• •

HISTORIC STRANAHAN HOUSE MUSEUM

ALONG THE NEW RIVER IN DOWNTOWN FORT LAUDERDALE STANDS THE HISTORIC STRANAHAN HOUSE MUSEUM, A TESTAMENT TO THE CITY'S BEGINNINGS AND THE VISIONARY PIONEERS WHO TRANSFORMED A FRONTIER TRADING POST INTO A THRIVING URBAN CENTER. AS THE OLDEST SURVIVING STRUCTURE IN BROWARD COUNTY, THE STRANAHAN HOUSE SERVES AS A REMINDER OF FORT LAUDERDALE'S PAST AND THE FOUNDATION OF ITS DEVELOPMENT.

MUSEUM OF DISCOVERY AND SCIENCE

THE MUSEUM OF DISCOVERY & SCIENCE (MODS) IS KNOWN AS SOUTH FLORIDA'S PREMIER SCIENCE CENTER, OFFERING VISITORS OF ALL AGES AN IMMERSIVE AND INTERACTIVE JOURNEY THROUGH THE WORLDS OF SCIENCE, TECHNOLOGY, AND NATURAL HISTORY. LOCATED IN DOWNTOWN ALONG THE RIVERWALK, THIS DYNAMIC INSTITUTION HAS EVOLVED FROM MODEST BEGINNINGS INTO A MAJOR EDUCATIONAL LANDMARK.

AS BOTH A TOURIST DESTINATION AND A VITAL EDUCATIONAL RESOURCE FOR SOUTH FLORIDA RESIDENTS, THE MUSEUM OF DISCOVERY & SCIENCE REPRESENTS A BRIDGE BETWEEN ENTERTAINMENT AND EDUCATION. THROUGH ITS CREATIVE EXHIBITS, CUTTING-EDGE IMAX THEATER, AND DIVERSE EDUCATIONAL PROGRAMS, MODS FULFILLS ITS MISSION OF CONNECTING PEOPLE TO INSPIRING SCIENCE, FOSTERING SCIENTIFIC LITERACY, AND ENCOURAGING DISCOVERY.

NSU ART MUSEUM FORT LAUDERDALE

SITUATED IN THE HEART OF DOWNTOWN FORT LAUDERDALE, THE NSU ART MUSEUM STANDS AS ONE OF SOUTH FLORIDA'S TOP CULTURAL INSTITUTIONS. THE NSU ART MUSEUM HAS A COMBINATION OF PERMANENT COLLECTIONS, ROTATING EXHIBITIONS, AND EDUCATIONAL PROGRAMMING TO CREATE A CITY CENTER FOR THE VISUAL ARTS THAT BRIDGES LOCAL AND GLOBAL ART COMMUNITIES.

Top Summer Fun Activities

HOW TO MAKE THE MOST OF SUMMER 2025 IN FORT LAUDERDALE

Hugh Taylor Birch State Park

Hugh Taylor Birch State Park stands is an 180-acre natural sanctuary sitting within the city landscape of South Florida. Often described as "Fort Lauderdale's Central Park," this park offers visitors a glimpse into Florida's natural ecosystems while providing recreational opportunities right outside of the city's famous beaches. Birch State Park offers recreational opportunities that take advantage of its natural setting:

- The park provides canoe and kayak rentals, allowing visitors to explore the waters of the Middle River, which flows through the western portion of the park. This waterway offers opportunities for viewing wading birds and occasionally manatees!

- A 2-mile paved path loops through the park. This loop is popular with walkers, joggers, and cyclists. For those seeking more nature, the Coastal Hammock Trail provides a mile-long hiking path through the maritime forest.

RENT WATER TOYS & SOAK UP THE SUN

Can you imagine the thrill of an electric surfboard, zipping through the waves? Or maybe you are more interested in the unique sensation of flyboarding, where you can soar above the water and dive beneath its surface.

For those who prefer a more calm experience, kayaking along the scenic Fort Lauderdale beach offers a peaceful escape from city life.

Aqua Flight provides a wide range of luxury water toys to yachts worldwide. Dedicated to offering you the utmost fun on board any boat, anywhere! Whether you are looking for adrenaline filled adventures or relaxing on a float lounging in the bay, or even want to charter a yacht, Aqua Flight provides it all

@AQUA_FLIGHT
754-300-1964
AQUA-FLIGHT.COM

AQUA FLIGHT

SNORKEL & DIVE FORT LAUDERDALE'S OFFSHORE REEFS

Fort Lauderdale offers incredible diving opportunities with its three-tiered reef system and numerous artificial reefs. Here's a guide to the top diving locations in the area:

Vista Park Reef
Location: Just offshore from Hugh Taylor Birch State Park
Depth: 15-30 feet (First Reef)
Highlights: Abundant tropical fish, nurse sharks, and sea turtles
Best for: Beginners and snorkelers due to shallow depth and typically gentle currents

The Ledge
Location: Second reef line, approximately 1/2 mile offshore
Depth: 40-50 feet
Highlights: Dramatic 15-foot drop-off, overhangs creating habitat for lobsters and moray eels
Best for: Intermediate divers comfortable with deeper depths

The Pillars
Location: Third reef, about 1 mile offshore
Depth: 60-70 feet
Highlights: Large coral formations resembling pillars, schools of pelagic fish
Best for: Advanced divers comfortable with deeper depths and occasional stronger currents

SS Copenhagen
Location: Off Lauderdale-by-the-Sea
Depth: 25-30 feet
Highlights: Historic 1900 shipwreck designated as an Underwater Archaeological Preserve
Best for: All certification levels, including snorkelers on clear days

Lady Luck
Location: 1.5 miles offshore
Depth: 120 feet
Highlights: 324-foot tanker intentionally sunk in 2016, featuring whimsical casino-themed art installations
Best for: Advanced divers and underwater photographers

Lauderdale-by-the-Sea
Location: Commercial pier area (Anglins Pier)
Depth: 10-15 feet
Highlights: Easy beach access to first reef, abundant marine life
Best for: Beginners, snorkelers, and those preferring shore diving to boats

SEE THE SIGHTS ON A SEGWAY TOUR

@SEGWAYFORTLAUDERDALE
954-304-5746
SEGWAYFORTLAUDERDALE.COM

SEGWAY FORT LAUDERDALE OFFERS SEVERAL SEGWAY TOUR OPTIONS THAT PROVIDE A UNIQUE AND EFFICIENT WAY TO EXPLORE THE CITY'S DIVERSE ATTRACTIONS. THESE GUIDED EXCURSIONS HAVE BECOME INCREASINGLY POPULAR AMONG VISITORS LOOKING FOR AN ALTERNATIVE TO TRADITIONAL WALKING OR BUS TOURS.

ARE YOU THINKING ABOUT TAKING A SEGWAY TOUR IN FORT LAUDERDALE? THIS TOP RATED ACTIVITY ON TRIPADVISOR.COM WILL HAVE YOU BLOWN AWAY! NO BALANCE, COORDINATION, OR EXPERTISE NEEDED, AND WE WILL MAKE YOU A PRO WITHIN MINUTES! YACHT/MANSION & NATURE PARK TOURS, AVAILABLE 7 DAYS A WEEK!

Ride. Explore. Discover.

BEAT THE HEAT AT THE BAPTIST HEALTH ICEPLEX

In a region known for its tropical climate and beach culture, the Baptist Health Iceplex is a unique recreational destination in Fort Lauderdale. This state-of-the-art ice sports facility offers South Florida residents and visitors the opportunity to experience ice-based activities year-round, regardless of the outdoor temperature.

The facility offers a wide range of programming for ice sports enthusiasts of all ages and skill levels including: Learn to Skate Programs, Hockey Development, Figure Skating & public sessions.

CHARTER A BOAT & SPEND A DAY ON THE WATER

Chartering a boat in Fort Lauderdale transforms a normal vacation into an extraordinary adventure. The extensive waterways, ideal temperatures, sand dunes to explore, and unmatched marine infrastructure create a boating experience that few destinations can rival. Whether you're seeking relaxation, adventure, or a connection to local culture, a Fort Lauderdale boat charter delivers an experience that simply cannot be replicated on land.

One fantastic boat charter service in Fort Lauderdale is Sunset Charter Services! Whether you're an experienced boater or a first-timer, Sunset Charter Services makes it easy to have an adventure you'll never forget. Food catering also available!

@SUNSETCHARTERSERVICES 336-501-7377
SUNSETCHARTERSERVICES.COM

SUNSET CHARTER
S E R V I C E S

Must Try Food

THE DINING EXPERIENCES & FOOD THAT MAKE FORT LAUDERDALE SPECIAL

LOCATED AT THE EDGE OF THE INTRACOASTAL WATERWAY IN FORT LAUDERDALE'S FAMOUS LAUDERDALE MARINA, 15TH STREET FISHERIES HAS STOOD AS AN ICONIC SEAFOOD DESTINATION FOR OVER FOUR DECADES. THIS RESTAURANT COMBINES FRESH SEAFOOD, WATERFRONT VIEWS, AND MARITIME HISTORY TO CREATE ONE OF FORT LAUDERDALE'S MOST SIGNATURE DINING EXPERIENCES.

ONE OF THE MOST BELOVED TRADITIONS AT 15TH STREET FISHERIES IS THE OPPORTUNITY TO FEED THE MASSIVE TARPON THAT GATHER AT THE DOCKS. THESE IMPRESSIVE SILVER FISH, SOME WEIGHING OVER 100 POUNDS, HAVE BECOME A FAMOUS ATTRACTION. FOR A SMALL FEE, VISITORS CAN PURCHASE FISH FOOD TO TOSS TO THE TARPON, CREATING MEMORABLE MOMENTS ESPECIALLY POPULAR WITH FAMILIES AND CHILDREN. THIS TRADITION CONNECTS DINERS TO THE MARINE ENVIRONMENT THAT MAKES FLORIDA SPECIAL.

café Bastille

by Bae

DEAL

15% OFF FINAL BILL

DEAL

Café Bastille is known as one of the best brunch restaurants, breakfast café', French bakery and juice places in both Fort Lauderdale & Miami, Florida. We proudly serve breakfast, lunch, brunch, fresh baked bread, pastries, delicious coffee, tea, fresh juices and wine all day every day of the week!

NO CASH VALUE
Valid June 1 – August 31, 2025
VOID IF STAMPED, SIGNED OR DETATCHED

- @CAFEBASTILLEMIAMI
- WWW.CAFEBASTILLEDOWNTOWN.COM
- 786-425-3575
- 704 SE 1st St, Fort Lauderdale

Nubé

ROOFTOP

LOCATED ATOP THE 26TH FLOOR OF THE HILTON FORT LAUDERDALE BEACH RESORT, NUBÉ ROOFTOP IS A TOP-TIER ROOFTOP BAR IN FORT LAUDERDALE BEACH. THIS ROOFTOP LOUNGE OFFERS PANORAMIC VIEWS OF THE OCEAN AND SKYLINE, PROVIDING THE PERFECT BACKDROP FOR A NIGHT OUT. WHETHER YOU'RE ENJOYING CRAFT COCKTAILS AT THE LUNAR BAR OR INDULGING IN CHEF-CURATED SHAREABLE PLATES, NUBÉ ROOFTOP BLENDS THE ATMOSPHERE OF A ROOFTOP RESTAURANT WITH THE RELAXED VIBE OF A COCKTAIL BAR. EXPERIENCE A UNIQUE "LOUNGE-AURANT" EXPERIENCE WITH INDOOR AND OUTDOOR SEATING, A WRAPAROUND GLASS BALCONY, AND VANISHING WALLS THAT ENHANCE THE INCREDIBLE ROOFTOP VIEWS. THIS IS ONE OF THE BEST DINING EXPERIENCES FORT LAUDERDALE HAS TO OFFER! RESERVATIONS ARE RECOMMENDED.

@NUBE_ROOFTOP

NUBEROOFTOP.COM

954-525-6823

505 N FORT LAUDERDALE BEACH BLVD 26TH FLOOR, FORT LAUDERDALE

DEAL

THE HOUSE ON THE RIVER IS A HISTORIC OASIS WHERE PEOPLE CAN EAT, DRINK, AND CELEBRATE DAY OR NIGHT IN TRUE FLORIDA RIVIERA STYLE, LOCATED DIRECTLY ON THE NEW RIVER IN THE HEART OF DOWNTOWN FORT LAUDERDALE. THIS ICONIC STRUCTURE IS COMPLEMENTED BY A CHARMING USE OF VINTAGE FURNITURE WITH A WHIMSICAL TWIST, OUTFITTED WITH MIXED CHINA, VIBRANT FLOWERS, AND SHADING TREES. THE RESTAURANT ALSO FEATURES EXTENSIVE OUTDOOR PATIO SEATING SET UNDER UMBRELLAS, MAKING THE HOUSE THE PERFECT WATERFRONT DESTINATION IN FORT LAUDERDALE.

@THEHOUSEONTHERIVERFL
THEHOUSEONTHERIVER.COM
954-825-2929
301 SW 3RD AVE, FORT LAUDERDALE

The
House
ON THE RIVER

TIMBR

Located on Las Olas Boulevard in Fort Lauderdale, TIMBR is a restaurant like no other! TIMBR is a fully immersive yet comfortable dining experience. TIMBR features "Vineyard Cuisine," a fusion of New American and European favorite dishes, made with locally sourced ingredients, all prepared with warmth and beauty. Our food and craft cocktails are both delicious and inventive. Enjoy everything from the finest prime steaks, seafood, and unique gourmet dishes to the greatest artisanal burgers, handmade pizzas, pastas, and pastries, in our two dining rooms, The Parc and The Atrium. On the 2nd floor, TIMBR features a small plate menu in our sexy and seductive lounge for a complete evening of delights.

@TIMBR_RESTAURANT

WWW.TIMBR-RESTAURANT.COM

954-787-5449

15 West Las Olas Blvd, Fort Lauderdale

Wild Thyme

OCEANSIDE EATERY

@WILDTHYMEFL

WILDTHYMEOCEANSIDE.COM

954-567-8070

601 N Fort Lauderdale Beach Blvd, Fort Lauderdale

WILD THYME OCEANSIDE EATERY OFFERS A GROWN-UP INTERPRETATION OF A BOARDWALK DINING EXPERIENCE WITH A REFRESHING TWIST ON FRESH DINING FAVORITES FROM THE LAND AND THE SEA. AT WILD THYME, GUESTS WILL ENJOY STUNNING, PANORAMIC OCEANFRONT VIEWS TO ACCOMPANY THEIR FRESH CAUGHT OCEAN AND FARM RAISED MAINLAND OFFERINGS. WILD THYME'S ECLECTIC MENU AND CHARMING BEACHFRONT AMBIANCE PROVIDES AN OCEANSIDE HOME ON FORT LAUDERDALE BEACH FOR LOCALS AND VISITORS ALIKE.

HAPPENING THIS SUMMER
IN FORT LAUDERDALE

STARLIGHT MUSICALS

EACH SUMMER, THE CITY OF FORT LAUDERDALE PARKS AND RECREATION DEPARTMENT PROUDLY PRESENTS THE BANK OF AMERICA STARLIGHT MUSICALS CONCERT SERIES. FOR 45 YEARS, THESE FREE OUTDOOR CONCERTS HAVE PROVIDED A GREAT WAY TO ENJOY THE SUMMER WITH FAMILY AND FRIENDS.

FRIDAYS, JUNE 6 – AUGUST 8, 2025 @ 7-10PM

HOLIDAY PARK - 1114 NE 12TH AVE, FORT LAUDERDALE

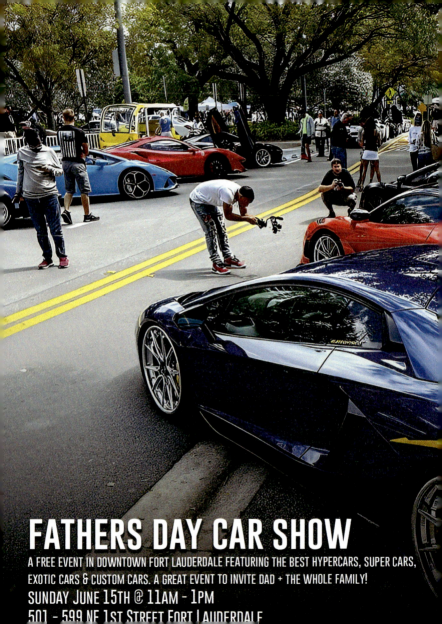

FATHERS DAY CAR SHOW

A FREE EVENT IN DOWNTOWN FORT LAUDERDALE FEATURING THE BEST HYPERCARS, SUPER CARS, EXOTIC CARS & CUSTOM CARS. A GREAT EVENT TO INVITE DAD + THE WHOLE FAMILY!

SUNDAY JUNE 15TH @ 11AM - 1PM

501 - 599 NE 1ST STREET FORT LAUDERDALE

RIVERWALK TACOS & TEQUILA FESTIVAL

THIS VIBRANT EVENT IS A CELEBRATION OF BOLD FLAVORS, FEATURING AN ARRAY OF DELICIOUS TACOS FROM LOCAL VENDORS AND A DIVERSE SELECTION OF PREMIUM TEQUILAS TO SAMPLE.

SATURDAY JULY 19TH @ 2-6PM

ESPLANADE PARK - 400 SW 2ND ST, FORT LAUDERDALE

4TH OF JULY SPECTACULAR

This Independence Day Celebration will feature a patriotic extravaganza, live bands, a kids zone, beach games, contests, family activities, and a dazzling fireworks display.

Friday July 4th @ 12 - 9:15pm
3000 E Las Olas Blvd, Fort Lauderdale

VEGAN BLOCK PARTY

Vegan Food, Drink, + Lifestyle Festival

Saturday July 5th @ 3-9PM

Esplanade Park - 400 SW 2nd St, Fort Lauderdale

RALLY LOUD

The young adult movement of First Baptist Fort Lauderdale. This 3 night event is free to atten and will feature powerful worship, an encouraging message, an afterparty, DJ & free food! July 24-26th – Follow @RALLYNIGHTS on Instagram for times & location

DINE OUT LAUDERDALE

Visit Lauderdale's Dine Out Lauderdale Restaurant Months showcases Greater Fort Lauderdale's diverse culinary offerings to residents and visitors.
See VISITLAUDERDALE.COM/DINEOUT for details

August 1 through September 30, 2025

SUMMER JAMZ

SUMMER JAMZ MARKS THE END OF SUMMER WITH THE HOTTEST CONCERT YOU DON'T WANT TO MISS INCLUDING HEADLINING ARTISTS AS WELL AS LOCAL FAVORITES.

FRIDAY AUGUST 15TH @ 7-10PM

MILLS POND PARK - 2201 NW 9TH AVE, FORT LAUDERDALE

The Pre Labor Day Festival

A BLOCK PARTY FEATURING LIVE MUSIC, A CAR SHOW, AS WELL AS FOOD AND DRINK SPECIALS FROM MORE 15 RESTAURANTS AND BARS.

SUNDAY AUGUST 31ST @ 10AM-9PM

NE 32ND ST AND NE 33RD ST FROM A1A WEST TO THE INTRACOASTAL

EXPERIENCE THE BEST THE CITY HAS TO OFFER!

THIS BOOK CAN SAVE YOU BIG **$$$!**
THANK YOU TO THE 60+ LOCAL BUSINESSES
COLLABORATING TO OFFER YOU FREEBIES,
DEALS & DISCOUNTS AROUND THE CITY.

TAKE ADVANTAGE! TRY SOMETHING NEW.
ALL DEALS & DISCOUNTS EXPIRE:

AUGUST 31, 2025

BARKYARD & BREWS

BarkYard n' Brews is one of South Florida's first off-leash Dog Park, Beer and Wine Bar. Conveniently located in Fort Lauderdale FL, just off of I-95. BarkYard n' Brews was started to create a safe and fun environment to promote the socialization between humans and their dogs. All patrons are welcome at Barkyard n' Brews, but a membership is required for all of our dog patrons. Your monthly or yearly annual membership helps us to ensure all dogs are healthy, up to date with vaccines, friendly and non-aggressive. We also offer Daily Dog Passes and anyone without a dog is more than welcome to visit free of charge. You do not need to bring a dog, you just have to like them!

@BARKYARDNBREWS

BARKYARDNBREWS.COM

954-530-3189

817 NW 1st St, Fort Lauderdale

511 Bar & Lounge

A local hangout for craft cocktails, great Happy Hour, rotating food trucks and live music. Outdoor games such as pool tables & cornhole. A great place to bring friends (and dogs!) for regular events. 511's unique cocktails, designed by Owner Trenton O'Connor, are blended from scratch by our awesome bar staff, and we offer a selection of locally brewed beers served up in frozen glasses.

@511bar_

511bar.com

954-401-0450

511 NE 3rd Ave, Fort Lauderdale

511
BAR & LOUNGE

PIZZA CRAFT PIZZERIA

Located in the historic Himmarshee District of Fort Auderdale, Pizza Craft is a cozy Italian restaurant, serving old school Italian specialties and award-wining wood fired-pizzas (Barstool rated 8.1). Pizza Craft is the perfect pot for a family dinner or a late-night rendezvous. Behind a air of doors inside, you'll find a hidden speakeasy-style ocktail bar called The Apothecary 330."

@PIZZACRAFT_PIZZERIA

PIZZACRAFTPIZZERIA.COM

954-616-8028

330 HIMMARSHEE ST #1, FORT LAUDERDALE

PIZZA ★ CRAFT
EST. 2015

MITCH'S DOWNTOWN BAGEL CAFE

MITCH'S IS A MODERN TAKE ON THE CLASSIC NEW YORK-STYLE DELI. WE SPECIALIZE IN BREAKFAST AND LUNCH, SERVED IN A VIBRANT, HOSPITALITY-DRIVEN ENVIRONMENT WHERE EVERY GUEST FEELS LIKE FAMILY. FROM ICONIC STAPLES LIKE MATZO BALL SOUP, LATKES, AND FRESH-BAKED BAGELS TO CRAVE-WORTHY ORIGINALS LIKE OUR HANGOVER SANDWICHES, WRAPS, AND FRENCH TOAST BITES, MITCH'S REDEFINES WHAT A DELI CAN BE—ROOTED IN TRADITION, ELEVATED FOR TODAY.

@MITCHSBAGELS   MITCHSDOWNTOWN.COM
954-779-7599   540 N ANDREWS AVE, FORT LAUDERDALE

MITCH'S
BAGEL   CAFE
DOWNTOWN

MISO Japanese Tapas

"MISO Japanese Tapas, opened in May 2023, brings a modern twist to Japanese cuisine. Fort Lauderdale residents can enjoy a delectable fusion of fresh seafood, sushi and ramen alongside an exciting tapas menu, perfect for sharing with friends or indulging solo."

@MISO_FTL

MISOJT.COM

954-530-3351

815 NE 2nd Ave, Fort Lauderdale

047

DOWNTOWN CHRISTIAN ACADEMY

DEAL

THE MISSION OF THE DOWNTOWN CHRISTIAN ACADEMY IS TO BE THE PREMIER CHILDCARE AND EDUCATION CENTER IN THE FORT LAUDERDALE COMMUNITY, SERVING CHILDREN FROM INFANTS THROUGH 5TH GRADE. WE PROVIDE A SAFE, HEALTHY, NURTURING, AND CREATIVE LEARNING ENVIRONMENT THAT CELEBRATES DIVERSITY AND INSPIRES A LOVE FOR LEARNING AT EVERY STAGE OF DEVELOPMENT.

@DCAFTL

DOWNTOWNCHRISTIANACADEMY.COM

954-713-7003   416 NE 1ST ST, FORT LAUDERDALE

DOWNTOWN
CHRISTIAN ACADEMY

Elba Las Olas

@ELBALASOLAS

ELBALASOLAS.COM

954-530-7319

250 SE 6TH AVE,
FORT LAUDERDALE

WITH AN ELEVATED RESTAURANT AND COCKTAIL BAR LOCATED IN THE HEART OF LAS OLAS, EXPERIENCE MEDITERRANEAN FLAVORS INSPIRED BY GREEK, FRENCH, NORTH AFRICAN, AND MIDDLE EAST CUISINES. ELBA LAS OLAS FEATURES A CAREFULLY CRAFTED FOOD MENU ALONG WITH WEEKEND BRUNCH, AN EXTENSIVE WINE LIST, AND DELICIOUS HANDCRAFTED COCKTAILS.

PLANTA

PLANTA QUEEN BRINGS BOLD FLAVOR AND FORWARD-THINKING INNOVATION TO THE HEART OF PLANT-BASED DINING. THE MENU FEATURES CRAVEABLE SUSHI, CUSTOMIZABLE BOWLS, AND PROTEIN-FORWARD DISHES THAT CATER TO EVERY CRAVING—FROM SIGNATURE CLASSICS TO FRESH NEW CREATIONS. ALL OF IT IS SERVED IN A HIGH-ENERGY, BEAUTIFULLY DESIGNED SPACE OVERFLOWING WITH FUN AND LATE-NIGHT VIBES.

WHETHER IT'S A QUICK LUNCH, A HAPPY HOUR, OR A NIGHT OUT, EVERY VISIT IS A CELEBRATION OF HOW FAR PLANTS HAVE COME—AND WHERE THEY'RE GOING NEXT.

@PLANTA   PLANTARESTAURANTS.COM
754-732-1952   1201 E LAS OLAS BLVD, FORT LAUDERDALE

EL TAQUITO

El Taquito in Fort Lauderdale brings the authentic taste of Mexico to the beachside. El Taquito's menu features classic Mexican dishes, from flavorful tacos to refreshing margaritas, all made with fresh high-quality ingredients. Located across from the ocean, we offer a vibrant atmosphere perfect for any occasion. Whether you're stopping by after a day at the beach or planning a special event, our dedicated team ensures a warm and friendly experience. We also provide catering services, bringing the best of Mexican cuisine to your gatherings. Visit us and enjoy the true flavors of Mexico!

@ELTAQUITOATTHEBEACH

ELTAQUITOMEXICANRESTAURANT.COM

754-206-2044

917 N Fort Lauderdale Beach Blvd, Fort Lauderdale

Ozzie's Restaurant Bar

Ozzie's Restaurant Bar was born out of a passion for blending the best of Italian and American cuisine. Located on Fort Lauderdale Beach, their mission is to offer a dining experience that combines exceptional flavors with a relaxed, inviting atmosphere. We believe in creating memorable moments through great food, excellent service, and a stunning seaside setting.

@ozziesrestaurantbar_

ozziesrestaurantbar.com

954-626-0049

905 N Fort Lauderdale Beach Blvd, Fort Lauderdale

052

CYCLEBAR FORT LAUDERDALE

WHETHER YOU ARE AN INDOOR CYCLING PRO OR ENTIRELY NEW TO THE EXPERIENCE, CYCLEBAR OFFERS ENERGIZING RIDES TAILORED TO ALL FITNESS LEVELS. CYCLEBAR WILL INSPIRE, MOTIVATE AND INVIGORATE YOU SO THAT YOU CAN FACE YOUR DAY. CYCLEBAR OFFERS AN INCLUSIVE AND INSPIRING LOW-IMPACT/HIGH-INTENSITY INDOOR CYCLING EXPERIENCE FOR ALL AGES AND BODY TYPES. NO MATTER WHERE YOU ARE IN YOUR FITNESS JOURNEY, THEIR CLASS EXPERIENCE PROMISES TO CALM YOUR MIND, ELEVATE YOUR MOOD AND REVIVE YOUR SENSES.

📷 @CYCLEBAR_FORTLAUDERDALE 🌐 WWW.CYCLEBAR.COM/LOCATION/FORT-LAUDERDALE

📞 984-342-4604 📍 525 N FEDERAL HWY SUITE 100, FORT LAUDERDALE

JETSET
MODERN PILATES

DEAL

🅞 *@JETSETPILATESFTL*

🌐 *JETSETPILATES.COM/FL/FLAGLER-VILLAGE/*

📞 *954-296-7307*

📍 *421 NE Sixth St, Suite 110, Fort Lauderdale*

JETSET Pilates Flagler Village offers a 50-minute full-body workout on our custom-designed JETSET reformers. Our modern Pilates method fuses high-intensity, low-impact movements with Pilates inspired exercises — designed to sculpt, tone, and energize the entire body. Each class is thoughtfully crafted with seamless transitions between exercises to keep your muscles under constant tension for maximum results. Led by expert instructors, every class is intentional, efficient, and open to all fitness levels — you'll never experience the same JETSET class twice!

McSorley's Beach Pub & Rooftop

📷 @MCSORLEYS_FTL 🌐 MCSORLEYSFTL.COM

📞 954-565-4446

📍 837 N Fort Lauderdale Beach Blvd, Fort Lauderdale

Located on A1A facing the beach. McSorley's is a two-story venue with 40+ TVs between 3 bars - a beach pub, an upstairs lounge & a rooftop deck Showing Live sports daily, including NFL, College Football, Premier League, UFC, Rugby, MLB, NHL, NBA, Champions League, Golf & Boxing. Live music, karaoke & DJs scheduled every week. We have a wide selection of beer, wine, cocktails, frozen drinks & food. Come by & check us out, whether you're looking for a pub, a sports bar or a rooftop drink in the sun! We're confident you'll be back! Can't find parking? Sonesta Hotel located next door offers valet 7 days a week!

McSorley's
BEACH PUB & ROOFTOP

THE GREEN TORTUGA COFFEE CO.

DEAL

LOCATED ACROSS FROM FORT LAUDERDALE BEACH.
WE PRIDE OURSELVES ON PROVIDING SPECIALTY
COFFEE. IRISH CHARM IN EVERY CUP, GREEN TORTUGA
COFFEE IS WORTH SLOWING DOWN FOR.

@GREENTORTUGACOFFEE

837 N FORT LAUDERDALE BEACH BLVD, FORT LAUDERDALE

GREEN TORTUGA

- C✿FFEE CO -

PADRINO'S CUBAN RESTAURANT

PADRINO'S RESTAURANTS IS A THIRD-GENERATION, FAMILY-OWNED CUBAN RESTAURANT WHERE TRADITION MEETS INNOVATION. INSPIRED BY OUR GRANDMOTHER'S RECIPES, OUR FATHER'S PASSION FOR SERVICE, AND OUR OWN DRIVE TO HONOR THEIR LEGACY WHILE GROWING SOMETHING NEW, WE OFFER BOLD CUBAN FLAVORS, HANDCRAFTED COCKTAILS, AND WARM HOSPITALITY IN A VIBRANT, MODERN SETTING.

WELLS COFFEE

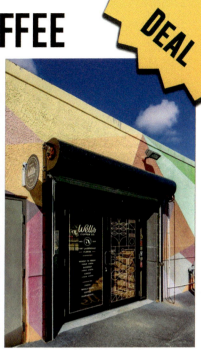

WELLS COFFEE CO. IS A SPECIALTY COFFEE ROASTER AND COFFEE BAR WITH TWO LOCATIONS IN DOWNTOWN FORT LAUDERDALE. WE SERVE EXCEPTIONAL, HAND-ROASTED COFFEE IN A RELAXED, FAMILY- AND DOG-FRIENDLY ATMOSPHERE—COMPLETE WITH FREE WI-FI. OUR EXPERT TEAM ROASTS SPECIALTY-GRADE COFFEES IN-HOUSE EVERY WEEK TO ENSURE PEAK FRESHNESS AND FLAVOR. COME BY, SIP A FRESHLY BREWED BEVERAGE, ENJOY A DELICIOUS LOCAL PASTRY, AND TAKE HOME A BAG OF YOUR FAVORITE COFFEE.

@WELLSCOFFEES   WELLSCOFFEES.COM

954-982-2886   737 NE 2ND AVE, FORT LAUDERDALE

954-533-2287   599 SW 2ND AVE, FORT LAUDERDALE

Patio Bar & Pizza

At Patio Bar & Pizza, Fort Lauderdale's newest hot spot for casual dining, you'll discover a vibrant ambiance that seamlessly blends the cozy feel of a neighborhood bar with the energy of a sports bar, all within a beautifully designed space. Indulge in signature brick-oven pizza, complemented by oven-fired wings, craft cocktails, local and imported beers, wine, and premium spirits. With happy hour specials until 7 PM and various events scheduled throughout the week, Patio Bar & Pizza is your go-to spot for a memorable dining experience in the heart of Fort Lauderdale."

 @PATIOBARPIZZA

 PATIOBARPIZZA.COM

 954-740-6000

901 Progresso Dr, Fort Lauderdale

PATIO

BAR & PIZZA

TULIO'S TACOS

Tulio's Tacos and Tequila Bar is a captivating bar and restaurant that transports patrons to the heart of Mexico's vibrant culinary and social traditions. Nestled in the charming community of Wilton Manors, Florida.

@TULIOSTACOS   TULIOSTACOS.COM

954-530-5523   2150 Wilton Dr, Wilton Manors

TULIO'S
TACOS & TEQUILA BAR

SISTRUNK MARKETPLACE

AND FOOD HALL

SISTRUNK MARKETPLACE IS A VIBRANT HUB IN FORT LAUDERDALE'S ART DISTRICT, BRINGING TOGETHER A DIVERSE CULINARY & SOCIAL SCENE UNDER ONE ROOF. ESTABLISHED IN 2020, IT HOUSES A VARIETY OF FOOD OPTIONS, CHOPS + HOPS AXE THROWING, RETRO VIDEO GAMES, DARTS AND POOL. SISTRUNK MARKETPLACE OFFERS AN EXCITING ATMOSPHERE TO EXPLORE AND SAVOR. THIS IS THE PERFECT PLACE TO BRING FRIENDS & BE SOCIAL!

@SISTRUNKMARKETPLACE 🌐 SISTRUNKMARKETPLACE.COM
📞 954-329-2551 📍 115 NW 6TH ST, FORT LAUDERDALE

Tarpon River Brewing

Tarpon River Brewing was originally an 11,000 square foot horse barn, called the Snyder Stables built in 1929. In this historic space, a 1000 square foot house was built within the infrastructure to create a compelling and comfortable taproom, tasting room, brewery, and kitchen. This home away from home, includes a full brewing system just outside the tasting room in full view for their patrons to see as they enjoy the atmosphere with a beer in hand.

Their tap list is as diverse as the owners of the brewery and range from golden ales to hoppy IPAs, dark lagers to fruited sours, and big stouts to wild ales. They offer beers that satisfy everyone from the beginner beer drinker to the eccentric beer snob.

@TARPONRIVERBREWING

TARPONRIVERBREWING.COM

954-353-3193

280 SW 6TH ST,
FORT LAUDERDALE

DEAL

1 Free beer

*NO CASH VALUE
VALID JUNE 1 - AUGUST 31, 2025
VOID IF STAMPED, SIGNED OR DETATCHED
RECIPIENT MUST BE 21 YEARS OF AGE OR OLDER

CON MURPHY'S
FORT LAUDERDALE BEACH

THE AWARD WINNING IRISH PUB FROM PHILADELPHIA HAS BROUGHT ITS SECOND LOCATION TO THE BEAUTIFUL BEACH FRONT PROPERTY IN FORT LAUDERDALE. CONVENIENTLY LOCATED IN BEACH PLACE, CON MURPHY'S OFFERS A VARIETY OF IRISH CLASSICS SUCH AS SHEPHERDS PIE, GUINNESS BEEF STEW, FISH & CHIPS, AND AMERICAN FAVORITES THAT INCLUDE SEAFOOD, STEAKS, PIZZA, TASTY SANDWICHES AND MORE. AT THE BEAUTIFULLY APPOINTED BAR THEY OFFER A GREAT BEER SELECTION INCLUDING ROTATING CRAFT BEERS ON TAP, AN EXTENSIVE COCKTAIL LIST WITH FROZEN DRINKS, AND SOME VERY TASTY WINES ON OFFER. CON'S IS A GREAT STOP, MAKE IT YOURS!

@CONMURPHYSFORTLAUDERDALE   CONMURPHYSFL.COM
954-686-2699   17 S FORT LAUDERDALE BEACH BLVD, FORT LAUDERDALE

CON MURPHY'S
OCEAN BAR & GRILL

BODEGA
Taqueria y Tequila

:camera: @BODEGAFLL

:globe: BODEGATAQUERIA.COM

:phone: 954-945-5545

:pin: 21 W LAS OLAS BLVD, FORT LAUDERDALE

FOUNDED IN SOUTH BEACH IN 2015, BODEGA TAQUERIA Y TEQUILA OFFERS AN ARRAY OF MEXICAN STREET FOOD ALONG WITH A UNIQUE NIGHT-LIFE EXPERIENCE SERVING UP AWARD-WINNING TEQUILA AND COCKTAILS. THE MEXICAN-INSPIRED CONCEPT FEATURES AN EXTENSIVE MENU SHOWCASING AUTHENTIC MEXICAN FAVORITES ALONG WITH UNCONVENTIONAL AND INNOVATIVE INTERPRETATIONS. SINCE ITS INCEPTION, BODEGA TAQUERIA Y TEQUILA HAS BEEN NATIONALLY RECOGNIZED AND REVERED AS ONE OF THE REGION'S HOTTEST CULINARY AND NIGHT-LIFE DESTINATIONS.

Hatch Brunch

IT'S MORE THAN JUST BRUNCH. HATCH IS HERE TO CHANGE THE PERCEPTION OF THE TYPICAL BRUNCH. IT'S ABOUT LIVING IN THE MOMENT, THE START OF A GREAT DAY AND CONNECTING WITH FRIENDS AND OUR COMMUNITY. SURPRISING TAKES ON BRUNCH CLASSICS ARE SERVED WITH A CONTAGIOUS PASSION FOR LIFE AND SERVING OTHERS.

 @HATCHBRUNCH

 754-200-8747

 HATCHBRUNCH.COM

 715 N FEDERAL HWY, FORT LAUDERDALE

HATCH

PEACE, LOVE & BACON

sana.

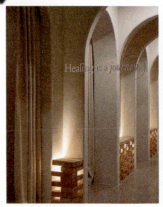
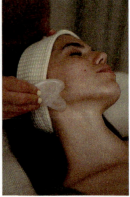

SANA IS A SKIN STUDIO MADE FOR YOU. WE ARE REDEFINING THE SKINCARE EXPERIENCE THROUGH GOAL DRIVEN FACIALS, REAL GUIDANCE AND CLEAN SKINCARE. MORE THAN A SKIN STUDIO, SANA IS A MOVEMENT TOWARDS HEALTHIER SKIN AND SELF LOVE.

- @SANASKINSTUDIO
- SANASKINSTUDIO.COM
- 954-944-3311
- 807 NE 2ND AVE SUITE 320, FORT LAUDERDALE

CITY CAVE

FLOAT & WELLNESS SPA

"Escape the pressures of daily life and immerse yourself in a world of pure relaxation at City Cave Float & Wellness Spa Flagler Village. Our sanctuary offers a unique combination of float therapy, infrared saunas, and massage therapies, catering to your mind, body, and soul. Float therapy allows you to float in a weightless environment, promoting stress reduction and muscle relaxation. Our infrared saunas gently heat your body, boosting your circulation and immune system. And our skilled massage therapists will pamper you with relaxation, deep tissue, and pregnancy massage sessions, leaving you feeling refreshed and rejuvenated.

[Instagram] @CITY.CAVE.FLAGLER.VILLAGE

[Web] CITYCAVE.COM

[Phone] 754-663-2283

[Location] 625 E Sunrise Blvd, Fort Lauderdale

LEGCY

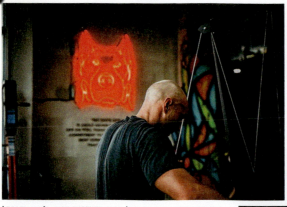

Legacy isn't just another gym. It is a community that is united by the unrelenting commitment to self-improvement. It doesn't matter how much money you have, where you've been, or what you look like. If you're dedicated to showing up, making the effort, and improving yourself so that you can serve and inspire those around you, then you are living a No Days Off lifestyle. And our training system, PIT, will get you in the best shape of your life.

@LEGACYFITFLL   LEGACYFIT.COM
305-302-4502   500 S Andrews Ave, Fort Lauderdale

LAS OLAS YOGA STUDIO

WE ARE A FORT LAUDERDALE YOGA STUDIO IN THE HEART OF DOWNTOWN ON LAS OLAS BLVD. AT LAS OLAS YOGA, OUR MISSION IS TO CREATE A SANCTUARY OF WELL-BEING, WHERE MOVEMENT, MINDFULNESS, AND COMMUNITY INTERSECT. WE PROVIDE A WELCOMING ENVIRONMENT WHERE YOU CAN RECONNECT WITH OLD FRIENDS, FORGE NEW CONNECTIONS, AND PRACTICE TOGETHER AS A SUPPORTIVE COMMUNITY. ALL OF OUR CLASSES ARE TAUGHT IN A NON-HEATED ENVIRONMENT, ALLOWING YOU TO FULLY IMMERSE YOURSELF IN THE PRACTICE WITHOUT EXTERNAL DISTRACTIONS.

@LASOLASYOGASTUDIO LASOLAS.YOGA

954-372-5275 1263 E LAS OLAS BLVD # 204, FORT LAUDERDALE

THE TERRACE GRILL

Terrace Grill, located in the heart of Fort Lauderdale, offers a sophisticated dining experience blending modern American cuisine with a coastal flair. Known for its elegant ambiance and stylish décor, the restaurant is a go-to destination for exceptional dishes crafted from fresh, local ingredients. Whether you're indulging in a leisurely brunch, a memorable dinner, or craft cocktails at the bar, Terrace Grill promises impeccable service and an inviting atmosphere. Perfect for intimate gatherings, celebrations, or a relaxed night out, Terrace Grill sets the standard for dining in Fort Lauderdale

@THETERRACEGRILL

THETERRACEGRILL.COM

954-945-9300

299 N Federal Hwy, Fort Lauderdale

THE
terrace
GRILL

ROSE'S COFFEE BAR

A SWEET SPOT FOR COFFEE, PRESSED JUICE, AND FRESH HOUSE MADE PASTRIES. ROSE'S WILL SERVE UP LA COLOMBE COFFEE, DEDICATED TO DELIVERING AN ELEVATED COFFEE EXPERIENCE. COMPLIMENTARY 30 MINUTE PARKING"

📷 @ROSESCOFFEEBAR

🌐 ROSESCOFFEEBAR.COM

📞 954-945-9500

📍 299 N FEDERAL HWY, FORT LAUDERDALE

SIDEWALK BOTTLESHOP

DEAL

SIDEWALK BOTTLE SHOP IS A NATURAL WINE BAR AND BOTTLE SHOP LOCATED IN FORT LAUDERDALE'S PROGRESSO NEIGHBORHOOD AT 901 PROGRESSO DRIVE. IT SPECIALIZES IN NATURAL WINES AND WAS ESTABLISHED IN 2021 AS A BOUTIQUE WINE SHOP THAT TURNS INTO A WINE BAR AT NIGHT.

JOIN THE SIDEWALK BOTTLESHOP WINE CLUB AND DISCOVER A CURATED SELECTION OF NATURAL WINES HANDPICKED BY FORT LAUDERDALE'S TOP NATURAL WINE SOMMELIERS, DAVID LOPEZ AND WALTER NAVARRO. ENJOY EXCLUSIVE ACCESS TO UNIQUE WINES, EXPERTLY SELECTED FOR THEIR QUALITY AND CHARACTER, DIRECTLY FROM ONE OF THE BEST IN THE INDUSTRY.

 @SIDEWALK.BOTTLESHOP

 SIDEWALKBOTTLESHOP.COM

954-744-0591

901 PROGRESSO DR
FORT LAUDERDALE

1 FREE GLASS OF WINE

*NO CASH VALUE
VALID JUNE 1 - AUGUST 31, 2025
VOID IF STAMPED, SIGNED OR DETATCHED
RECIPIENT MUST BE 21 YEARS OF AGE OR OLDER

Luxury Air Tours

See Fort Lauderdale from the sky! Relish in a top-of-the-line aircraft featuring panoramic views, reclined seating fabricated with a luxurious interior. Marvel in the best views and feel comfortable along the way – courtesy of Luxury Air Tours highly experienced pilots and their expertise of South Florida.

@LUXURYAIRTOURS   FLYLUXEAIRTOURS.COM
561-802-7720   1525 NW 56TH STREET , FORT LAUDERDALE

LUXURY AIR TOURS
OF SOUTH FLORIDA

075

PONTOON PARTY

Owned and operated by Florida natives, Pontoon Party is your #1 destination for an amazing day on the water. Our mission is simple: deliver outstanding service and make sure that every customer has a great time. Our pontoon boats are large, comfortable, seaworthy and the perfect platform to throw your next party! Mix drinks, sun on the top deck, play in the water with our inflatables and just generally have a great time with Pontoon Party. Experienced captains will take you through the sights of South Florida, know all the best bars, and are friendly and knowledgeable. And remember, it's your pontoon and your party!

@PONTOONPARTYFORTLAUDERDALE ⊕ PONTOONPARTY.COM

833-476-6866 ⊗ 1401 SE 15TH ST, FORT LAUDERDALE

Pontoon Party

˙FORT

Welcome to The Fort. Your premier destination for Pickleball enthusiasts featuring 43 professional regulation courts and the world's first dedicated Pickleball stadium. Our state of the art facility is perfect for casual and competitive players. Experience open play, skill-rated reserve play, leagues, tournaments, and lessons with our pro staff. Rain or shine, 14 of our courts are weatherproof ensuring uninterrupted play. With onsite pro shop, locker rooms, beach club, bar and food, there's something for everyone at The Fort!

50% OFF DAY PASS

*NO CASH VALUE
VALID JUNE 1 - AUGUST 31, 2025
VOID IF STAMPED, SIGNED OR DETATCHED

⊙ @PLAYTHEFORT
🌐 PLAYTHEFORT.COM
📞 954-222-1965
📍 891 SW 34TH ST, Fort Lauderdale

OutFit®

OutFit is a full body strength workout that includes elite cardio conditioning and optimizes your caloric burn in a motivating supportive community in an amazing outdoor environment. OutFit's mission is to deliver to communities across the country an exquisite, boutique exercise experience that is convenient, fun, and which average folks can actually afford.

Why OutFit?

Outdoor Experience: Inspiring workouts in beautiful outdoor spaces

Expert-Led: Professional coaches delivering high-quality Functional Interval Training (FIT)

Flexible Formats: Options for group classes, personal training, and customized programs

Affordable: Low-cost monthly subscriptions with flexible membership options

@OUTFITTRAINING_HQ   OUTFITTRAINING.COM
954-678-3444   Multiple locations

COYO TACO

FORT LAUDERDALE'S FRESHEST MEXICAN STREET FOOD EXPERIENCE! AT COYO TACO, GUACAMOLE IS SMASHED TO ORDER AND TORTILLAS ARE HANDCRAFTED ON-SITE IN AN AUTHENTIC MEXICAN TRADITION. VEGETABLES ARE FARM FRESH AND RESPONSIBLY SOURCED. MEAT AND SEAFOOD ARE NATURALLY RAISED AND HUMANELY TREATED. AGUA FRESCAS AND MARGARITAS ARE MADE FROM SCRATCH. STAYING TRUE TO OUR TODO FRESCO, OR 'EVERYTHING FRESH' PHILOSOPHY, OUR INGREDIENTS ARE 100% NATURAL. THE COYO TACO BRAND HAS A SIGNIFICANT SOCIAL MEDIA PRESENCE WITH 60K FOLLOWER' ON INSTAGRAM, AND LOCATIONS IN WYNWOOD, BRICKELL, CORAL GABLES, LAS OLAS, AND SOUTH MIAMI, AS WELL AS INTERNATIONAL LOCATIONS IN THE DOMINICAN REPUBLIC, COLOMBIA, AND PORTUGAL.

@COYOTACO
COYO-TACO.COM
954-766-1292
401 E LAS OLAS BLVD #150, FORT LAUDERDALE

Johnny's Hungry Hoagies

DEAL

T Johnny's Hungry Hoagies, our mission is to craft gourmet oagies that delight taste buds with the freshest, meticulously liced meats, cheeses, and crisp vegetables. Complemented by ourmet salads and world-class coffee options, we aim to elevate he hoagie experience, offering a symphony of flavors in every bite hile ensuring a commitment to quality and customer atisfaction.

@JOHNNYS_HUNGRY_HOAGIES

JOHNNYSHUNGRY.COM

858-462-4437

790 East Broward Blvd,
Fort Lauderdale

HUNGRY HOAGIES

Johnny's

HUNGRY HOAGIES

Boathouse At The Riverside

Situated directly on the New River, Boathouse at the Riverside offers an amazing waterfront experience with the best views in downtown Fort Lauderdale. Our local & international inspired cuisine menu features plenty of healthy options and salad choices. Every table offers breathtaking views of the yachts and boats cruising the New River. Enjoying a beautiful day on the water? Dock and Dine with us! We feature a variety of small, medium, and large plates in a casual, family-friendly atmosphere. Fort Lauderdale locals and travelers alike to enjoy handcrafted cocktails, beer and wine in a casual waterfront dining setting. Whether you are looking to grab a quick bite or wine and dine on the waterfront, Boathouse is the perfect choice.

@BHRIVERSIDE   BOATHOUSERIVERSIDE.COM
954-377-5494   620 SE 4TH ST, FORT LAUDERDALE

BOATHOUSE
AT THE RIVERSIDE

RIVERSIDE HOTEL

From quaint rooms with a charming, vintage feel to spacious suites featuring sensational views, the Riverside Hotel provides some of the most comfortable accommodations in Fort Lauderdale. Each of our 231 rooms and suites is designed for today's savvy traveler. Embrace the Florida ambiance of our Classic Tower rooms or unwind from the day with city-lights and Intracoastal Waterway views from our Junior Suite Rooms built in 2001. The ambiance of these rooms are elegant and spacious. Enjoy sensational views of the Fort Lauderdale skyline and the New River.

@RIVERSIDEHOTELFL
RIVERSIDEHOTEL.COM
954-467-0671
620 E Las Olas Blvd, Fort Lauderdale

RIVERSIDE HOTEL
ON LAS OLAS BOULEVARD

Est. 1936

WILD SEA LAS OLAS

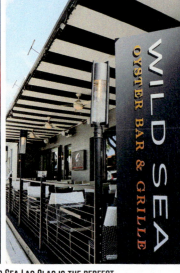

OVERLOOKING FORT LAUDERDALE'S LAS OLAS BOULEVARD, WILD SEA LAS OLAS IS THE PERFECT RESTAURANT FOR SAVORING DELICIOUS CUISINE AT AFFORDABLE PRICES. ENJOY BREAKFAST, LUNCH, BRUNCH, & DINNER IN AN UPBEAT, CHIC AND CONTEMPORARY AMBIANCE WHILE WATCHING LIFE GO BY ON ONE OF THE TRENDIEST THOROUGHFARES IN FORT LAUDERDALE. THE MODERN AMBIANCE OF OUR RESTAURANT REFLECTS THE UPSCALE ENERGY OF LAS OLAS BOULEVARD, WITH THE INDOOR DINING SPACE FEATURING CHIC FURNISHINGS AND DESIGNER TOUCHES. GUESTS MAY ALSO DINE ON THE SIDEWALK TERRACE WHICH OFFERS A GREAT SPOT FOR PEOPLE-WATCHING. LOCATED IN THE HISTORIC RIVERSIDE HOTEL, WILD SEA LAS OLAS IS A FAVORITE GATHERING PLACE AMONG VISITORS AND FORT LAUDERDALE LOCALS ALIKE."

@WILDSEALASOLAS   WILDSEALASOLAS.COM

954-467-2555   620 E LAS OLAS BLVD, FORT LAUDERDA

WILD SEA

LAS OLAS

New River Cafe & Bakery

ET IN ONE OF THE BEST LOCATIONS NEAR
ORT LAUDERDALE'S FASHIONABLE LAS OLAS
OULEVARD, NEW RIVER CAFÉ & BAKERY
ELIGHTS YOUR SWEET TOOTH WITH
ROM-SCRATCH BAKED CUSTOM CAKES,
RTISAN BREAD, SWEET TREATS, HOMEMADE
AMS, PANINIS, GRAB-AND-GO OPTIONS AND
ESSERTS THAT ARE DELICIOUS AND IN-
PIRED. EXECUTIVE PASTRY CHEF SABRINA
ND HER TEAM COMBINE THEIR CREATIVITY,
ASSION, AND TECHNIQUE TO CRAFT EVERY
ECIPE – FROM INNOVATIVE BAKERY ITEMS
O TASTY BREAKFAST AND LUNCH FAVORITES
IKE PIPING HOT BACON, EGG AND CHEESE
REAKFAST BUNS, PANINIS, AND MORE."

@NEWRIVERCAFEBAKERY
NEWRIVERCAFEANDBAKERY.COM
954-377-5500
420 SE 6TH AVE, FORT LAUDERDALE

DEAL

COMPLIMENTARY FRESHLY BREWED ICED TEA OR COLD BREW WITH ANY $5 PURCHASE.

*NO CASH VALUE
VALID JUNE 1 - AUGUST 31, 2025
VOID IF STAMPED, SIGNED OR DETATCHED

084

DOWNTOWN EVENT CENTER

LOCATED IN THE HEART OF THE CITY OF FORT LAUDERDALE, THE DOWNTOWN EVENT CENTER IS A PREMIER VENUE FOR HOSTING A WIDE ARRAY OF EVENTS, FROM CORPORATE MEETINGS AND CONFERENCES TO WEDDINGS AND COMMUNITY GATHERINGS. OUR STATE-OF-THE-ART FACILITIES AND EXCEPTIONAL SERVICES MAKE US THE PERFECT CHOICE FOR ANY OCCASION, ENSURING AN UNFORGETTABLE EXPERIENCE FOR ALL ATTENDEES."

@FTLEVENTCENTER FTLDOWNTOWNEVENTCENTER.COM
954-831-1142 416 NE 1ST ST, FORT LAUDERDALE

DOWNTOWN
EVENT CENTER

HUGH'S CATERING

UGH'S CULINARY IS A PREMIER ULL-SERVICE CATERER, OFF-SITE VENT CREATOR AND PRIVATE VENUE ASED OUT OF FORT LAUDERDALE, LORIDA. FOR OVER 40+ YEARS WE AVE ESTABLISHED OURSELVES AS ONE F SOUTH FLORIDA'S LEADING CULINARY XPERTS, PROUDLY SERVING BROWARD OUNTY AND TRI-COUNTY AREAS VE'LL WORK WITH YOU EVERY STEP OF HE WAY, OFFERING CUSTOMIZED MENU ND BAR PACKAGES, SERVICE STAFF, ENTAL EQUIPMENT, ENTERTAINMENT, LORALS/DÉCOR AND FULL PRODUCTION.

@HUGHSCULINARY   HUGHSCATERING.COM

954-563-4844   4351 NE 12TH TERRACE, OAKLAND PARK

10% OFF ANY CATERING PACKAGE

*NO CASH VALUE
VALID JUNE 1 - AUGUST 31, 2025
VOID IF STAMPED, SIGNED OR DETATCHED

TEMPLE STREET EATERY

Temple Street Eatery is your go-to neighborhood Asian American restaurant, established in 2014. We specialize in fast, friendly service and a casual dining experience that highlights global street food with a local twist. Our menu features a diverse range of homemade daily specials—from fresh salads and inventive sandwiches to delightful small bites, savory dumplings, and hearty bowls and soups. Each dish is crafted to offer comfort with a touch of culinary adventure. Join us to explore new flavors and rediscover familiar favorites as we enlighten your palate.

:camera: @TEMPLESTREETEATERY :globe: TEMPLESTREETEATERY.COM
:phone: 754-701-0976 :pin: 416 N Federal Hwy, Fort Lauderdale

Bandoleros Tacos & Tequila Bar

DEAL

Located in the Historic District in Downtown Fort Lauderdale, Bandoleros Tacos is a fresh take on Mexican food. Walking distance from Broward Center & Revolutions Live. We use fresh made tortillas for all our tacos, quesadillas and burritos. We serve classic tacos but also fusion tacos with flavorful combinations. Paring any of the food items with our Tequila & Mezcal list with fresh fruit cocktails is a perfect combination for any occasion.

 @BANDOLEROSTACOS

 BANDOLEROSTAQUERIA.COM

 786-913-9307

208 SW 2ND ST, FORT LAUDERDALE

DEAL

1 Free Appetizer

*NO CASH VALUE
VALID JUNE 1 - AUGUST 31, 2025
VOID IF STAMPED, SIGNED OR DETATCHED

Pause Fort Lauderdale

Pause is an experiential wellness studio that offers modern services that boost immunity and support physical, mental, and emotional recovery to help you move better, sleep better, work better, feel better, and live better"

📷 @PAUSEFTL

🌐 PAUSESTUDIO.COM

📞 754-228-6784

📍 2071 E Oakland Park Blvd, Oakland Park

CLEAN YOUR DIRTY FACE

CLEAN YOUR DIRTY FACE® STUDIOS FOCUS ON FACIALS ONLY AND IS THE BEST PLACE TO RECOVER FROM A DAY IN THE SUN AND A NIGHT OF FUN! BE PREPARED TO RECEIVE PERSONALIZED, PROFESSIONAL SKINCARE IN A FRIENDLY + FUN SETTING. WE STRIVE FOR EFFICIENCY, EFFECTIVENESS, AND EDUCATION, WITH EACH FACIAL TAKING UNDER 30 MINUTES. OUR LICENSED ESTHETICIANS WILL STEAM, DEEP CLEAN, EXFOLIATE, MASK, TONE AND MOISTURIZE WITH HIGH-QUALITY, CLEAN, NON-TOXIC SKINCARE PRODUCTS WHILE OUR SIGNATURE 5-POINT ACUPRESSURE FACE MASSAGE WILL HELP WITH BLOOD CIRCULATION, LYMPHATIC DRAINAGE AND RELAXATION.

@CLEANYOURDIRTYFACE

CLEANYOURDIRTYFACE.COM

561-663-4855

902 N FLAGLER DR, FORT LAUDERDALE

RUMBLE BOXING
FORT LAUDERDALE

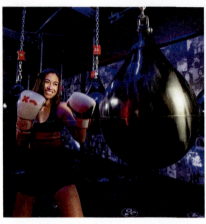

@RUMBLEBOXINGFORTLAUDERDALE

RUMBLEBOXINGGYM.COM

954-859-6067 408 NE 3RD ST, FORT LAUDERDALE

RUMBLE BOXING FORT LAUDERDALE DELIVERS BOXING & STRENGTH GROUP FITNESS WORKOUTS FOR ALL FITNESS LEVELS. OUR BOXING-INSPIRED FITNESS BOUTIQUE COMBINES THE SWEET SCIENCE OF BOXING WITH THE TRANSFORMATIVE POWER OF STRENGTH TRAINING IN ONE SEAMLESS CLASS. EACH 10-ROUND CLASS IS AN EXPLOSIVE, FULL-BODY WORKOUT WITH HIIT, METABOLIC CONDITIONING, AND STRENGTH & CARDIO CIRCUITS. REAP REWARDS IN EVERY ROUND® AND RUMBLE AT YOUR OWN PACE."

KIDS HIDEOUT

KIDS HIDEOUT IS NOT YOUR TYPICAL INDOOR PLAYGROUND, OUR INDOOR PLAY CITY WAS INTENTIONALLY DESIGNED TO ENHANCE CREATIVITY AND SKILLS THROUGH PRETEND PLAY, ART AND SENSORY PLAY, WHILE KEEPING KIDS AWAY FROM TECHNOLOGY AND OVERSTIMULATING ENVIRONMENTS. WE BELIEVE THAT THROUGH PLAY CHILDREN LEARN ABOUT THEIR WORLD, EXPLORE, AND INTERACT WITH EACH OTHER WHILE PERFORMING DIFFERENT JOBS AND ACTIVITIES, AND THEY PERFORM BETTER WHEN THEY ARE FOCUSED AND HAVING FUN.

THIS SPACE IS HIGHLY RECOMMENDED FOR CHILDREN UP TO 8, AND IT IS A SAFE ENVIRONMENT WHERE YOUNGER KIDS CAN PLAY AND WONDER FREELY. OUR SMALL SPACE ALLOWS CHILDREN TO DEVELOP THEIR SENSE OF INDEPENDENCE, WHILE PARENTS CAN RELAX AND ENJOY THEIR TIME WHILE KNOWING THAT THEIR CHILDREN ARE HAVING FUN AND DEVELOPING SKILLS.

@KIDS.HIDEOUT

KIDSHIDEOUT.COM

754-202 8332

1495 N FEDERAL HWY, FORT LAUDERDALE

20% OFF ENTRY

*NO CASH VALUE
VALID JUNE 1 - AUGUST 31ST 2025
VOID IF STAMPED, SIGNED OR DETATCHED

SAPIDO ITALIAN

Sapido is a modern Italian restaurant and pizza, wine and cafe. All the products are authentic from Italy and everything is made with traditional recipes. We are the place to go for fresh daily homemade Italian food such as Pasta, Gnocchi, Lasagna, Meat, Fish, Authentic Pizza, Fresh Salads, Italian Wine and Coffee. Join us for lunch or dinner and enjoy authentic Italia food prepared by a team of chefs directly from Italy. We also offer catering for private and corporate events. Come and visit us, you will feel like you just flew to Italy!

@SAPIDORESTAURANT   SAPIDOGROUP.COM
954-488-8000   111 SE 8TH AVE, FORT LAUDERDALE

SÀPIDO
RISTORANTE ITALIANO
EST. 2015

THE DEN SPORTS BAR AND LOUNGE

THE DEN IS A TRENDY SPORTS BAR WITH A LARGE BEER SELECTION AND CRAFT COCKTAILS, PLUS HAPPY HOUR SPECIALS. IT'S THE PERFECT PLACE TO CATCH A GAME & BRING FRIENDS FOR A FUN NIGHT OUT!

◎ @THEDENFTL

⊕ THEDENFTL.COM

📞 754-216-2736

📍 201 SW 2ND ST, FORT LAUDERDALE

The Den
SPORTS BAR & LOUNGE

REST ASSURED ROOFING CORP.

DEAL

REST ASSURED ROOFING IS A FAMILY OWNED AND OPERATED STATE LICENSED ROOFING CO, WITH OVER 30 YEARS OF EXPERIENCE IN THE ROOFING INDUSTRY. WE PRIDE OURSELVES IN PROVIDING OUR CUSTOMERS WITH OUTSTANDING SERVICE THROUGHOUT THE ENTIRE PROCESS. FROM THE SALE OF THE JOB THROUGH COMPLETION AND 100% CUSTOMER SATISFACTION. ONLY TOP-GRADE MATERIALS ARE USED FOR EACH JOB, WHICH ALLOWS US TO GUARANTEE OUR CUSTOMERS THEY ARE GETTING A TOP-QUALITY ROOF. REST ASSURED ROOFING IS A FULL-SERVICE ROOFING COMPANY SERVICING FORT LAUDERDALE

 @RESTASSUREDROOFINGCORP 🌐 WWW.RESTASSUREDROOFS.COM

📞 954-303-7443

DEAL

$200 OFF A ROOF REPAIR

*NO CASH VALUE
VALID JUNE 1 - AUGUST 31, 2025
VOID IF STAMPED, SIGNED OR DETATCHED

DEAL

$500 OFF A RE-ROOF

*NO CASH VALUE
VALID JUNE 1 - AUGUST 31, 2025
VOID IF STAMPED, SIGNED OR DETATCHED

FLANIGAN'S

FLANIGAN'S IS A LAIDBACK FAMILY-RUN RESTAURANT ANCHORED BY A COMMITMENT TO EXCEPTIONAL FOOD AND DRINK, WARM HOSPITALITY, GREAT VALUE, AND GOOD FUN. A BELOVED SOUTH FLORIDA INSTITUTION SINCE 1959, THE FLANIGAN'S NAME IS PRETTY MUCH SYNONYMOUS WITH GOOD TIMES. THE FOUNDING VISION OF JOE "BIG DADDY" FLANIGAN — A COME ONE, COME ALL, HOME-AWAY-FROM-HOME FOR FRIENDS OLD AND NEW — IS ALIVE AND WELL TODAY. OVER THE YEARS, FLANIGAN'S EVOLVED FROM POPULAR BIG DADDY'S LOUNGES AND LIQUOR STORES INTO A GROUP OF OVER 20 RESTAURANTS. THE DESIGN OF OUR BARS AND RESTAURANTS IS ALL ABOUT THE ISLAND VIBES AND SALTWATER ADVENTURES THAT REFLECT OUR DEEP SOUTH FLORIDA ROOTS. AND, OH YEAH, THOSE LEGENDARY BABY BACK RIBS...

@FLANIGANSFL

FLANIGANS.NET

954-791-3942

2600 DAVIE BLVD, FORT LAUDERDALE

FLANIGAN'S IS A BELOVED FAN FAVORITE BY THE LOCALS OF THE CITY OF FORT LAUDERDALE. THE MEMBERS OF REDDIT.COM/R/FORTLAUDERDALE KNOW.

JOIN THE FLAN CLUB FOR EXCLUSIVE DISCOUNTS

Notes

Notes

Thank You

THANK YOU TO THE MANY COLLABORATORS THAT HELPED MAKE THIS GUIDE BOOK A REALITY!

SPECIAL THANK YOU TO SUBLIME.IMAGERY ON INSTAGRAM FOR PHOTO SUPPORT

TO STAY CONNECTED TO WHAT IS HAPPENING WEEKLY IN FORT LAUDERDALE FOLLOW:

@FORTLAUDERDALEDOWNTOWN   @FORTLAUDERDALEGUIDEBOOK

ARE YOU A LOCAL FORT LAUDERDALE BUSINESS INTERESTED IN BEING FEATURED IN A FUTURE GUIDE BOOK?
EMAIL US AT:
HELLO@FORTLAUDERDALEGUIDEBOOK.COM